PRESIDENT GEORGE W. BUSH:

A REMARKABLE RECORD OF ACHIEVEMENT

AUGUST 2004

Table of Contents

INTRODUCTION

President George W. Bush's first term has been among the most consequential and successful in modern times. Under his leadership, the United States is waging and winning the war against global terrorism. The United States and its coalition partners liberated more than 50 million people from two regimes of extraordinary brutality that had provided safe haven to terrorists. And we are promoting democracy in regions of the world that have never known it.

The United States military is receiving the strongest support from a commander-in-chief in two decades. President Bush has taken unprecedented steps to stop the spread of weapons of mass destruction – and he has signed one of the most sweeping arms reduction pacts in history. America is in the process of deploying a missile defense that will help protect the United States and its allies from catastrophic attacks. President Bush signed into law landmark legislation that better prepares our defense establishment to meet the challenges of the 21st century – and he announced the most comprehensive restructuring of US military forces overseas since the end of the Korean War.

During his first term, President Bush has signed into law three major tax cuts, including the largest in two decades – and since the summer of 2003, America has had the fastest-growing economy of any major industrialized nation in the world. Under President Bush's leadership, the economy has been growing at rates as fast as any in nearly 20 years. The homeownership rate has been at a record high. Interest and mortgage rates have been near historic lows. The core rate of inflation over the past year ranks among its lowest in 40 years. The rate of growth of Federal spending is slowing, jobs are being created at a brisk pace (1.3 million jobs in the first six months of this year), and the unemployment rate today remains below the average unemployment rate of the 1970s, the 1980s, and the 1990s.

President Bush signed into law the No Child Left Behind Act, the most important Federal education reform in history, one that insists that testing, accountability, and high standards will accompany record new resources. Medicare has been modernized, prescription drug coverage has been added, and Americans now have the opportunity to use Health Savings Accounts, tax-free accounts designed to help individuals save for health expenses. Faith-based groups are receiving unprecedented support and encouragement. And President Bush signed into law the most far-reaching reform of American business practices since the time of Franklin Roosevelt.

To ensure the safety of our citizens, President Bush has implemented the most sweeping changes in the organization of our national security institutions since World War II. With the creation of the Department of Homeland Security, America has seen the most extensive reorganization of the Federal government since President Truman. President Bush has proposed the most thoroughgoing reorganization of the intelligence community in more than a half century. And thanks to the USA PATRIOT Act, Federal law enforcement agencies can better share information, track terrorists, and protect American lives.

President Bush has strongly advocated open markets for American goods; affordable, reliable, and secure energy supplies; and environmental standards that are making America's water and air cleaner. In the social realm, he has championed a culture of life and a new culture of responsibility; the strengthening and defense of marriage; judges who strictly and faithfully interpret the law; and stronger work requirements for welfare recipients. He has made civility a touchstone of his rhetoric. He has put together an Administration comprising enormously talented men and women – and one with more diversity in senior positions than any in history.

These achievements are anchored in a set of core beliefs: America is a defender and promoter of freedom – and the advance of freedom brings peace. We must lead the world with strength and confidence. Religion should not be banned from the public square. Government should encourage ownership and opportunity, compassion and responsibility. The proper role of government is to create the environment in which small business owners and entrepreneurs will take risks and invest, hire workers and spark economic growth.

The last four years have been a time of extraordinary challenges. They include the horrific terrorist attack on the American homeland; global wars; an economy that was sliding toward recession when President Bush took office; and the revelation of corporate scandals long in the making that undermined investor confidence.

Such times demand a leader of clear convictions and determination, hope and vision, integrity and the courage to act. These qualities are the hallmarks of the Bush Presidency. There is much that remains to be done – yet as this document illustrates, an enormous amount has already been accomplished. President George W. Bush put forward a historically ambitious agenda and restored dignity to the office he holds. He has provided steady leadership in the face of unprecedented challenges. The United States is safer and stronger, more resilient and better for his efforts.

WAGING AND WINNING
THE WAR ON TERROR

"Great harm has been done to us. We have suffered great loss. And in our grief and anger we have found our mission and our moment. Freedom and fear are at war. The advance of human freedom – the great achievement of our time, and the great hope of every time – now depends on us. Our nation – this generation – will lift a dark threat of violence from our people and our future. We will rally the world to this cause by our efforts, by our courage. We will not tire, we will not falter, and we will not fail." – President George W. Bush, September 20, 2001

THE ACCOMPLISHMENTS

Fighting Global Terrorism

- President Bush launched *a global effort to defeat terrorism and to protect and defend America*. During his term in office, the President has led a steady and systematic campaign against global terrorists and their allies.

- Since the terrorist attacks on September 11th, the United States has waged two of the swiftest and most humane wars in history (in Afghanistan and Iraq). *Fifty million people have been liberated from two of the world's most brutal and aggressive regimes* – and the terrorists' foreign operating bases are being taken away.

- *Massive damage has been inflicted on al Qaeda and its terror allies*. Of those directly involved in organizing the September 11th attacks, *almost all are now in custody or confirmed dead*.

- Of the senior al Qaeda and associated leaders, operational managers, and key facilitators the United States has been tracking, *more than two-thirds have been detained, captured, or killed*. These include Mohammed Atef, al Qaeda's senior field commander killed in a bombing raid in Afghanistan; Abu Zubaida, Osama bin Laden's field commander after the killing of Atef, captured in Pakistan; Khalid Sheikh Mohammed, mastermind of the September 11th attacks, captured in Pakistan; Ramzi Binalshibh, a coordinator of the September 11th attacks, captured in Pakistan; Hambali, top strategist for al Qaeda's associate group Jemaah Islamiah in Southeast Asia, captured in Thailand; Abd al-Rahim al-Nashiri, al Qaeda's chief of operations in the Persian Gulf, captured in the United Arab Emirates; Ahmed Khalfan Ghailani, a suspect in the 1998 bombings of the US embassies in Kenya and Tanzania, captured in Pakistan; and Abu Issa al–Hindi, a central planner of detailed reconnaissance of American financial institutions, captured in Britain.

- Operational and logistical *terrorist support cells have been disrupted* in Europe, Saudi Arabia, Yemen, and Southeast Asia.

- Nearly *$140 million in terrorist assets have been blocked in over 1,400 accounts worldwide*.

- We are working closely with intelligence services all over the globe and have *enhanced our intelligence capabilities* in order to trace dangerous weapons activity.

The War to Liberate Afghanistan

- In Operation Enduring Freedom, *the United States built a worldwide coalition of 70 countries that destroyed terrorist training camps, dismantled the brutal Taliban regime, denied al Qaeda a safe haven in Afghanistan, and saved a people from starvation.*

- Today, *Afghanistan has a new president, Hamid Karzai, and a new constitution that gives unprecedented rights and freedoms to all Afghans.*

- *Historic presidential and parliamentary elections are planned for this fall and the following spring.* America will launch an ambitious training program for newly-elected Afghan politicians.

- Preliminary figures indicate that *nearly nine million Afghan citizens (91 percent of the electorate) have so far registered to vote.*

- Three years ago, women in Afghanistan were whipped in the streets, executed in a sports stadium, and beaten for wearing brightly-colored shoes. Schooling was denied to girls. Today, *the constitution gives women the right to vote and guarantees freedom of expression, assembly, and religion.* Young girls are attending school. Two Afghan cabinet ministers are women, and a woman leads the Afghan Independent Human Rights Commission.

- One hundred forty-five health care facilities have been constructed or rehabilitated. *The coalition has trained thousands of Afghan health care professionals, treated 700,000 cases of malaria, and inoculated close to 4.5 million children against measles and other childhood diseases.*

- *More than 200 schools have been rebuilt; 7,000 teachers have been trained; and 25 million textbooks have been provided to Afghan students.*

- *The coalition is training a modern Afghan national army to defend its borders, root out terrorists, and promote national unity.* There are now close to 25,000 trained Afghan police officers and the Afghan police are on track to achieve their goal of up to 50,000 trained officers by December 2005.

The War to Liberate Iraq

- On March 19, 2003, the United States and its coalition partners launched Operation Iraqi Freedom. Three weeks later, *Saddam Hussein's regime was toppled from power.* Today the former dictator is awaiting trial in prison rather than ruling in a palace. A regional threat and state-sponsor of terrorism has been removed. Sovereignty has been transferred to the Iraqi people, and free elections will be held in January 2005.

- The international community has pledged at least $32 billion to *rebuild and improve schools, health care, roads, water, agriculture, electricity, and other elements of Iraq's infrastructure.*

- *Schools and clinics have been renovated and reopened, and power plants, hospitals, water and sanitation facilities, and bridges and roads are being rehabilitated.* Since the liberation of Iraq, food and electricity are now distributed more equally across the country.

- *Iraq's oil infrastructure is being rebuilt*, with production capacity reaching between 2.3 and 2.5 million barrels of oil per day.

- Saddam Hussein's regime spent $16 million in 2002 on health care – less than one dollar per Iraqi per year. *Iraq's budget for the Ministry of Health is now $950 million.*

- *More and more Iraqi children are attending schools.* Attendance in the 2003-2004 school year is as high as, or in some cases higher than, pre-conflict levels. More than eight million new textbooks have been distributed around the country.

- *Iraqi university students and scholars are now able to communicate and travel abroad freely*, reconnecting Iraqi higher education with the international academic community after decades of isolation.

- Iraqis now have an *ever-growing free press*, including newspapers, internet, radio stations, and satellite television networks.

- *Small businesses are opening in Iraq*, creating new jobs for Iraqis.

- *A year and a half ago, Iraq was an enemy of America and the civilized world; today it is an ally of both.*

Recruiting New Allies in the War on Terror

- Three years ago, Pakistan was one of the few countries in the world that recognized the Taliban regime, and al Qaeda was active and recruiting in Pakistan without serious opposition. *Today, the United States and Pakistan are working closely in the fight against terror*, and Pakistani forces are rounding up terrorists along the nation's western border.

- Three years ago, terrorists were established in Saudi Arabia. Inside that country, fundraisers and other facilitators gave al Qaeda financial and logistical help with little scrutiny or opposition. Today, after attacks in Riyadh and elsewhere, *Saudi Arabia is working to shut down the facilitators and financial supporters of terrorism*, and they have captured or killed many leaders of the al Qaeda organization in Saudi Arabia.

- Three years ago, Yemen stonewalled the investigation of the USS Cole bombing. Today, *Yemeni authorities have moved against al Qaeda in their own territory; hosted Army Special Forces to train and advise Yemeni troops in counterterrorism; and increased contacts with the Defense Department, CIA, and FBI.* In November 2002, Yemeni authorities allowed a US Predator drone to kill six al Qaeda operatives in Yemen, including senior al Qaeda leader Abu Ali al-Harithi.

- Indonesia, the world's largest Muslim country, *has moved against Jemaah Islamiah, the al Qaeda-linked Islamic terrorist organization*, and has arrested its suspected leader, radical cleric Abubakar Baasyir.

- The US military has *trained and advised Philippine troops in Philippine-led anti-terror operations*, such as those against the Abu Sayyaf Islamic terrorist group.

Halting the Proliferation of Weapons of Mass Destruction

- President Bush led the creation of the Proliferation Security Initiative (PSI), *a broad international partnership of more than 60 countries that is interdicting lethal materials in transit*. These nations are sharing intelligence information, tracking suspect international cargo, and conducting joint military exercises.

- As a result of the PSI, American and British intelligence discovered advanced components intended to build nuclear weapons that were being shipped to Libya. German and Italian authorities helped seize the materials. And confronted with the discovery, *Libya voluntarily agreed to end its WMD programs*.

- American and British intelligence officers *uncovered and shut down a sophisticated black market network* headed by A.Q. Khan, the architect of Pakistan's nuclear weapons program, which sold nuclear technologies and equipment to outlaw regimes stretching from North Africa to the Korean Peninsula.

- President Bush spearheaded the establishment of the G-8 Global Partnership, which over 10 years will *provide $20 billion in nonproliferation and weapons reduction assistance to the former Soviet Union*. This represents a dramatic increase in US and allied efforts.

- In the former Soviet Union, 41 percent of the 600 metric tons of weapons-usable material that was previously determined to be vulnerable has been secured. US-Russian efforts have shortened by two years the timeline for *securing weapons-usable nuclear material* at 51 sites in Russia and other former Soviet states.

- The Bush Administration launched the Megaports Initiative, a global nuclear material detection effort focused on major seaports to the United States. It is helping *stem illicit trafficking of nuclear and radiological materials*.

- Since 2001, the United States has installed radiation detection equipment at 39 Russian border sites to *deter and interdict trafficking in nuclear and radioactive materials*.

- President Bush proposed that only states that have signed the Additional Protocol – which *requires states to declare a broad range of nuclear activities and facilities and allows the International Atomic Energy Agency (IAEA) to inspect those facilities* – be allowed to import equipment for their civilian nuclear programs.

- The President has proposed the *creation of a special committee of the IAEA Board that will focus intensively on safeguards and verification*.

STRENGTHENING OUR MILITARY, SUPPORTING OUR VETERANS

"America today has the finest [military] the world has ever seen. And with your help, I am committing to ensuring that we have the world's finest [military] tomorrow and every day after. To do so, we must build forces that draw upon the revolutionary advances in the technology of war that will allow us to keep the peace by redefining war on our terms. I'm committed to building a future force that is defined less by size and more by mobility and swiftness, one that is easier to deploy and sustain, one that relies more heavily on stealth, precision weaponry and information technologies." – President George W. Bush, May 25, 2001

THE ACCOMPLISHMENTS

Strengthening our Military

- President Bush has increased defense spending by more than one-third – *the largest increase in a generation*.

- The President has *increased military research and development by more than 50 percent*.

- President Bush signed into law *landmark legislation that better prepares our defense establishment to meet the challenges of the 21st century*. A military that was designed for the challenges of the mid-to-late 20th century is being transformed into a lighter, more flexible, more agile, and more lethal force – one better able to deal with new threats to our national security.

- President Bush announced *the most comprehensive restructuring of US military forces overseas since the end of the Korean War*. By closing bases no longer needed to meet Cold War threats that have ended, this new initiative will bring home many Cold War-era forces while deploying more flexible and rapidly deployable capabilities in strategic locations around the world.

Deploying a Missile Defense

- The President has *doubled investment in a missile defense system*.

- The United States will *soon deploy a functioning missile defense system to protect Americans from nuclear threats posed by rogue regimes* – and will deploy the first land and sea-based system.

- The United States is acting with the support and cooperation of Australia, Britain, Japan, and other nations to establish a missile defense capability with *support sites on multiple continents*.

- The Department of Defense has conducted *several successful tests of a national missile defense system* in which an incoming missile was intercepted and destroyed.

Strengthening the NATO Alliance

- President Bush has been a leader in *transforming NATO* to make it effective in the 21st century and the global war on terror.

- In 2004, _NATO welcomed seven new members from Central and Eastern Europe into the Alliance_.

- NATO leaders and Russian President Vladimir Putin _created the NATO-Russia Council to facilitate consultation and joint action_.

- The Alliance commands the International Security Assistance Force (consisting of more than 6,000 troops) that is helping secure and rebuild a free Afghanistan. _Afghanistan is NATO's first mission outside of Europe_.

- _NATO allies are contributing troops to the coalition in Iraq_ and NATO leaders have agreed to help train Iraq's new security forces.

- NATO launched the Istanbul Cooperation Initiative, which will _increase cooperative security efforts with the broader Middle East_ in areas including counterterrorism and halting the proliferation of weapons of mass destruction.

- The United States proposed with Norway a measure to _adopt a "zero tolerance" policy on human trafficking_ in areas of NATO operations. NATO will develop specific measures to support local efforts to combat trafficking. Two hundred thousand victims of trafficking are transported through the Balkans each year, a region where NATO has a significant presence.

Supporting Military Families and Veterans

- Since President Bush took office, _basic pay for service members has increased by more than 20 percent_ – and the increase in payments for food and housing combined has reached 50 percent.

- _Funding for child care services has increased by $21.5 million_.

- The Military Family Tax Relief Act of 2003 provides _tax relief and other benefits to members of the armed services and their families_.

- President Bush has proposed _unprecedented levels of funding for veterans_. His 2005 budget represents an increase in overall funding for our nation's veterans by almost $20 billion – or 40 percent – since 2001. The President has increased funding for our veterans more in four years than funding was increased in the previous eight years.

- Since 2001, President Bush's four budgets for the Department of Veterans Affairs (VA) have _provided a more than 40 percent increase in veterans' medical care spending alone_.

- Changes have been implemented to _ensure that veterans receive timely, quality medical care_. Waiting lists for medical care have been essentially eliminated and the processing time for disability claims has been reduced by 30 percent.

- The President's budgets have allowed _2.5 million more veterans to enroll for health care_; outpatient visits to increase from 44 million to 54 million; the number of prescriptions filled to increase from 98 million to 116 million; and 194 new community-based clinics to open.

- President Bush has twice signed legislation effectively providing "concurrent receipt" of both _military retired pay and disability compensation for those military retirees most deserving_, combat injured and highly disabled, reversing a century-old law.

- *The President has committed $1.5 billion in his 2004 and 2005 budgets to increase outpatient health care services for veterans, to build new hospitals, and to modernize or replace outdated pre-World War II facilities.* Through the Capital Asset Realignment for Enhanced Services (CARES) plan, the VA is working to better distribute its network of clinics and hospitals so that the vast majority of veterans are within 30 miles of a VA community-based outpatient clinic or similar facility.

PROMOTING PEACE AND DEMOCRACY -
AND ACTS OF MERCY

"Sixty years of Western nations excusing and accommodating the lack of freedom in the Middle East did nothing to make us safe – because in the long run, stability cannot be purchased at the expense of liberty. As long as the Middle East remains a place where freedom does not flourish, it will remain a place of stagnation, resentment, and violence ready for export. And with the spread of weapons that can bring catastrophic harm to our country and to our friends, it would be reckless to accept the status quo. Therefore, the United States has adopted a new policy, a forward strategy of freedom in the Middle East. This strategy requires the same persistence and energy and idealism we have shown before. And it will yield the same results. As in Europe, as in Asia, as in every region of the world, the advance of freedom leads to peace. The advance of freedom is the calling of our time; it is the calling of our country." – President George W. Bush, November 6, 2003

THE ACCOMPLISHMENTS

Promoting Democracy

- Today, *more than fifty million people who lived under brutal and backward regimes in Afghanistan and Iraq are on the road to democracy*. Iraq is on its way to becoming the first democratic nation in the Arab Middle East.

- President Bush has made a *forward strategy of freedom in the Middle East* a cornerstone of his foreign policy. This means supporting the rise of democracy, and the hope and progress that democracy brings, as the alternative to hatred and terror.

- In 2004, President Bush led the G-8 in establishing *a historic partnership with the Broader Middle East and North Africa to advance freedom, democracy, and prosperity in the region*. The G-8 will expand their existing efforts and launch new initiatives to support democracy, literacy, entrepreneurship and vocational training, as well as small business financing and development.

- President Bush has proposed *doubling the budget of the National Endowment for Democracy* to focus its new work on the development of free elections, free markets, free press, and free labor unions in the Middle East.

- To cut through the barriers of hateful propaganda, *the Voice of America and other broadcast services are expanding their programming in Arabic and Persian*, and a new television service is providing news and information across the region.

Arms Control

- President Bush signed a treaty with Russia's President Vladimir Putin to *reduce nuclear stockpiles by two-thirds* over 10 years.

- The United States and its allies obtained a commitment from Libya to *abandon its chemical and nuclear weapons programs*.

- The United States and its allies *interrupted a production network of weapons parts for Libya, Iran, and North Korea*.

Averting Conflicts

- In 2002, _American diplomatic intervention helped defuse a possible nuclear conflict between India and Pakistan_.

- Through the President's initiative, the United States brought Japan, South Korea, China, and Russia to the table for discussions with North Korea on ending Pyongyang's nuclear weapons program. _This multilateral approach has increased pressure on Pyongyang to eliminate verifiably its nuclear weapons program_.

- In 2003, American diplomatic and military leadership _averted a greater conflict in Liberia_. The President approved the use of the American military to support an African security force in Liberia; helped ensure a peaceful transition of power; and is now providing needed resources to Liberia.

Combating the Global AIDS Pandemic

- In his 2003 State of the Union address, President Bush proposed the Emergency Plan for AIDS Relief, _a historic plan to address the AIDS pandemic_. This constitutes the largest single up-front commitment in history for an international public health initiative involving a specific disease.

- The President committed $15 billion, including $10 billion in new money, over five years to _treat at least two million patients with life-extending drugs and prevent seven million new infections_ in the most afflicted nations of Africa, Asia, and the Caribbean. His plan will also _care for 10 million HIV-infected and HIV-affected individuals, including AIDS orphans_.

- _During the last three years, America has given more international AIDS assistance than the rest of the world's donor governments combined_.

- President Bush led the G-8 effort to _establish a Global HIV Vaccine Enterprise to coordinate a worldwide effort to find an HIV vaccine_ and announced plans also to establish a second _HIV Vaccine Research and Development Center in the United States_. The United States is committed to spending over a half-billion dollars a year on vaccine research.

- The President has _emphasized the successful "ABC" (Abstain, Be Faithful, Use Condoms) approach in preventing the sexual transmission of AIDS_.

Providing Assistance to Nations in Need

- In March 2002, President Bush announced the Millennium Challenge Account, which proposed a 50 percent increase in America's core development assistance by 2006 and tied this record increase in aid to political, legal, and economic reforms in the recipient countries. _The Millennium Challenge Account provides the largest increase in US development assistance since the Marshall Plan_.

- The President has advanced a _nearly $1 billion initiative to provide clean drinking water to 50 million people in the developing world_. The Administration also proposed the Initiative to End Hunger in Africa by widening the use of new high-yield bio-crops.

- _President Bush signed an extended African Growth and Opportunity Act_ (AGOA), which has demonstrated the power of free markets to improve lives in both the United States and Africa. By reducing barriers to trade, the AGOA Acceleration Act will increase exports, create jobs, and *expand opportunity for Africans and Americans alike*. It gives American businesses greater confidence to invest in Africa, and encourages African nations to reform their economies and governments to take advantage of the opportunities that AGOA provides.

- Under the Trafficking Victims Protection Act, the United States is using sanctions against governments to discourage human trafficking. President Bush is committing $50 million to support the good work of organizations that are rescuing women and children from sexual slavery and slave labor, and giving them shelter, medical treatment, and the hope of a new life. *Since 2001 the Administration has provided more than $295 million to support anti-trafficking programs in more than 120 countries*.

PROTECTING THE HOMELAND

"As we wage this war abroad, we must remember where it began – here on our homeland. In this new kind of war, the enemy's objective is to strike us on our own territory and make our people live in fear. This danger places all of you, every person here and the people you work with, on the front lines of the war on terror. Our methods for fighting this war at home are very different from those we use abroad, yet our strategy is the same: We're on the offensive against terror. We're determined to stop the enemy before they can strike our people." – President George W. Bush, September 10, 2003

THE ACCOMPLISHMENTS

Improving Homeland Security

- With strong bipartisan support President Bush *created the Department of Homeland Security* – the most comprehensive reorganization of the Federal government in a half-century. The Department of Homeland Security consolidates 22 agencies and 180,000 employees, unifying once-fragmented Federal functions in a single agency dedicated to protecting America from terrorism.

- President Bush has *nearly tripled homeland security discretionary funding*.

- *More than $18 billion has been awarded to state and local governments to protect the homeland*.

- The Bush Administration developed a *comprehensive National Strategy for Homeland Security*, focused on six key areas: intelligence and warning; border and transportation security; domestic counterterrorism; protecting critical infrastructure; defending against catastrophic threats; and emergency preparedness and response.

- The Administration developed national strategies to help *secure cyberspace and the infrastructures and assets vital to our public health, safety, political institutions, and economy*.

- The President authorized the establishment of the United States Northern Command, to *provide for integrated homeland defense and coordinated Pentagon support to Federal, state, and local governments*.

- For the first time, the President has made *countering and investigating terrorist activity the number one priority for both law enforcement and intelligence agencies*. The Bush Administration has transformed the FBI into an agency whose primary mission is to prevent terrorist attacks and increased its budget by 60 percent.

Improving Intelligence

- *President Bush proposed the most thoroughgoing reorganization of the intelligence community in more than a half-century*. The President supports the creation of a *National Intelligence Director* to serve as his principal intelligence advisor. He will also establish a National Counterterrorism Center (NCTC) and strongly supports the 9/11 Commission's recommendations to reorganize congressional oversight for both intelligence and homeland security.

- In his 2003 State of the Union address, President Bush announced the _creation of the Terrorist Threat Integration Center_ (TTIC) to synthesize information collected within the United States and abroad about possible terrorist threats.

- The _Terrorist Screening Center (TSC) was launched_ to consolidate terrorist watch lists and provide continual operational support for Federal, state, and local screeners and law enforcement.

- The FBI has _established a new Executive Director for Intelligence and specially-trained intelligence analysts_.

- The Department of Homeland Security Information Network is connected to all 50 states and more than 50 major urban areas, and allows _information sharing among thousands of local agencies and the Homeland Security Operations Center_.

New Tools to Fight Terrorism

- President Bush won overwhelming support for the USA PATRIOT Act, a law that _gives intelligence and law enforcement officials important new tools to fight terrorists_. This legislation has prevented terrorist attacks and saved American lives.

- The dramatic increase in information sharing allowed by the PATRIOT Act has enabled law enforcement to _find and dismantle terror cells in Portland, Oregon; Lackawanna, New York; and Northern Virginia_.

- _Warrants are now applicable across state and district lines, eliminating the need to obtain multiple warrants for the same person_ – a lengthy process that previously hindered counterterrorism efforts.

- _Law enforcement officials have been given better tools to fight terrorism_, including roving wire taps and the capacity to seize assets and end financial counterfeiting, smuggling and money-laundering.

- Judges are now able to _impose stiffer sentences on terrorists_.

Supporting First Responders

- The President's 2005 budget reflects a _780 percent increase in funding for first responders_ since September 11th.

- Since September 11th, _more than a half-million first responders across America have been trained_.

- The Bush Administration has proposed _doubling the level of first responder preparedness grants_ targeted to high-threat urban areas. The Urban Area Security Initiative enhances the ability of large urban areas to prepare for and respond to threats or acts of terrorism.

Strengthening Defenses Against Biological, Chemical, and Radiological Weapons

- President Bush signed into law Project BioShield, _an unprecedented, $5.6 billion effort to develop vaccines and other medical responses to biological, chemical, nuclear, and radiological weapons_.

- The Bush Administration is _investing more than $7 billion across all aspects of biodefense_. In the last three years, the Administration has created the BioWatch program to monitor major cities for a biological release, procured sufficient smallpox vaccine for all citizens, and significantly increased stocks of antibiotics against anthrax.

- State and local health systems have been provided more than _$4.4 billion to bolster their ability to respond to public health crises_.

- The Bush Administration undertook several initiatives to _detect radiological materials being smuggled into our Nation_, issuing thousands of portable radiation detectors to border control personnel and installing radiation detection portals at ports of entry.

- _Security and research to protect the Nation's food supply from terrorists has increased_, adding millions of dollars in funding and hundreds of food inspectors.

Improving Aviation, Border, and Port Security

- To support improved border and transportation security, funding levels _have increased by $9 billion_ since September 11th.

- _Aviation security has been improved from the curb to the cockpit_. Hardened cockpit doors have been installed on all US commercial aircraft. Flight deck crews are being trained to carry guns in the cockpit. Thousands of air marshals are being deployed daily. All checked baggage now is being screened. And canine teams are now positioned at every major airport to search for explosives.

- Over the last three years, _nearly $15 billion has been devoted to strengthening aviation security_.

- The visa issuance process has been tightened to _better screen foreign visitors_; the US-VISIT program was created to use cutting-edge biometrics to check the identity of foreign travelers; and the Student and Exchange Visitor Information System was created to verify foreign student activity in the United States.

- _New Coast Guard vessels and specialized maritime security units have been added_.

- The Container Security Initiative was developed to _allow US inspectors to screen high-risk shipping containers at major foreign ports_ before they are loaded in ships bound for America.

- The National Targeting Center was created to vet passenger lists of aircraft and container shippers to identify high-risk individuals and shipments. Today, _100 percent of high-risk cargo containers are examined by US inspectors_.

Helping Victims of the September 11th Attacks

- The Administration implemented a _$40 billion emergency response package_ to begin the recovery from the attacks and to protect national security.

- President Bush signed legislation that _sped compensation to the family of each fallen police officer, firefighter, and rescuer_.

- The President, working closely with Congress, created the _September 11th Victim Compensation Fund_, which established a streamlined claim process for victims of the

September 11th attacks to receive compensation. The Fund will provide a total of about $7 billion in financial aid.

- More than 10,000 business owners across the Nation were approved for *more than $1 billion in disaster loans* to help deal with the economic consequences of the attacks.

ECONOMIC GROWTH AND
JOB CREATION

"Today we are taking essential action to strengthen the American economy.... We are helping workers who need more take-home pay. We're helping seniors who rely on dividends. We're helping small business owners looking to grow and to create more new jobs. We're helping families with children who will receive immediate relief. By ensuring that Americans have more to spend, to save, and to invest, this [tax relief] legislation is adding fuel to an economic recovery. We have taken aggressive action to strengthen the foundation of our economy so that every American who wants to work will be able to find a job." – President George W. Bush, May 28, 2003

THE ACCOMPLISHMENTS

A Growing Economy

- Since last summer, _the American economy has grown at the fastest rate of any major industrialized nation_.

- _America's economy has been growing at rates as fast as any in nearly 20 years_.

- _Nearly 1.5 million jobs have been created since August 2003_ and 1.3 million new jobs have been created this year alone. The unemployment rate today is *below* the average unemployment rate of the 1970s, the 1980s, and the 1990s.

- From 2000 to 2003, _productivity grew at the fastest three-year rate in more than a half-century_, raising the standard of living for all Americans.

- The Conference Board's index of leading indicators has risen at an average annual rate of 4.2 percent since March 2003 – the fastest 15-month period of increase in 20 years – _suggesting vibrant economic growth in the near term_.

- The stock market regained more than $4 trillion in equity since its low in mid-2002. _In 2003 the Dow Jones Industrial Average rose 25 percent and the NASDAQ rose 50 percent_.

- _Manufacturing activity expanded in July 2004 for the 14th consecutive month_.

- Real after-tax incomes are _up 11 percent_ since December 2000.

- Interest rates reached their _lowest levels in decades_ during the Bush Administration.

- _Homeownership reached an all-time high and mortgage rates reached their lowest level in decades_.

- During the Bush Administration, we have experienced one of the _lowest core inflation rates (averaging two percent per year) in the past 40 years_.

Historic Tax Relief

- President Bush, working closely with Congress, _provided the largest tax relief in a generation_.

- The President secured enactment of _three major tax relief bills_, providing tax relief to every taxpayer who pays income tax while completely eliminating the income tax burden for nearly five million families.

- In 2004, taxpayers will receive, _on average, a tax cut of $1,586_.

- _The marriage penalty for low and moderate income taxpayers has been reduced_. In 2004, 49 million married couples will receive an average tax cut of $2,602.

- _The child tax credit has been doubled, increasing from $500 to $1,000_. In 2004, 43 million families with children will receive an average tax cut of $2,090.

- _Twenty-five million small business owners will receive tax relief averaging $3,001_. The President's tax relief also provides America's businesses with incentives to invest in new equipment to make their workers more productive and to create new jobs.

- President Bush, working with Congress, _is phasing out the death tax_.

Providing Job Training

- President Bush proposed the _Jobs for the 21st Century initiative_, providing more than a half-billion dollars in funding for new education and job training initiatives. The plan includes $250 million to fund partnerships between community colleges and employers to help Americans prepare for the higher-skilled, higher-paying jobs of the new century, and $33 million for expanded Pell Grants for low-income students.

- The Bush Administration proposed _$23 billion for job training and employment assistance in 2005_.

- The President proposed a _$50 million Personal Reemployment Accounts pilot program_, allowing unemployed workers who have the hardest time finding jobs to choose the services they need to return to work, including assistance with training, child care, and transportation costs.

- President Bush has supported _extension of Federal unemployment benefits_ three times, providing more than $23 billion to help almost eight million American workers.

- President Bush proposed to _reform major Federal job training programs_ to double the number of people trained, and to ensure more people receive flexible Innovation Training Accounts which allow workers to make choices about the skills they need.

Helping America's Small Businesses

- President Bush's _historic tax relief_ reduced marginal income tax rates across-the-board, benefiting the more than 90 percent of small businesses that pay taxes at individual income tax rates. In 2004, 25 million small businesses will save, on average, $3,001 due to the President's tax relief.

- *President Bush raised from $25,000 to $100,000 the amount that small businesses can expense for new capital investments*, reducing the cost of purchasing new machinery, computers, trucks, and other qualified investments.

- *The number of women-owned businesses has continued to grow at twice the rate of all United States businesses*. Women are now the owners of 10.6 million businesses in the country, which generate $3.6 trillion in sales, and between 1997 and 2002, employment at majority-women-owned private companies increased by 30 percent.

- The Bush Administration *proposed and supports Association Health Plans* (AHPs) to help employees of small businesses afford health coverage.

- *The regulatory burden on small businesses has been reduced*. Small business owners have also been given a bigger voice on ways to improve regulations.

- The Administration has implemented *new regulations that help small businesses* compete for Federal procurement dollars and streamlined the appeals process.

Promoting Minority Small Businesses

- Business loans to minorities *increased by 40 percent* in 2003.

- President Bush proposed a *21 percent increase for the Minority Business Development Agency*, the largest increase in more than a decade.

Supporting Technological Innovation

- President Bush has proposed *the largest Federal research and development budget in history*.

- President Bush proposed *making permanent the research and experimentation tax credit* to promote private sector investment in new technologies and manufacturing techniques.

- The President created a *new math and science partnership program* to improve teacher training and student learning. The President's 2005 budget meets his commitment to fully fund his five-year, $1 billion goal.

- The Bush Administration set a national goal of *universal, affordable access to broadband technology* by the year 2007 – and it has opposed all efforts to tax access to broadband.

Restraining Federal Spending and Improving Government Efficiency

- President Bush *brought the annual rate of growth in non-security discretionary spending down* from 15 percent in the last budget enacted during the Clinton Administration to a proposed 0.5 percent for next year.

- The President's budget will put the country on a path toward *cutting the deficit in half* from its peak over the next five years. And better progress is being made than anticipated just six months ago. Rising revenues, spurred by a growing economy, are decreasing the deficit faster than anticipated.

- The Bush Administration launched the President's Management Agenda (PMA) to *make the Federal government more results-oriented and accountable*. For the first time, a majority of agencies evaluate their employees based on how well they are performing relative to clear expectations. Departments and agencies have assessed the performance of more than 600 programs, representing approximately $1.4 trillion in Federal spending, And by working to eliminate more than $35 billion in improper payments and producing more timely and accurate financial information, more Federal agencies than ever are being held accountable for spending the taxpayers' money wisely.

- The Bush Administration has achieved *the biggest overhaul of the Federal civil service system in a quarter-century* and opened up hundreds of thousands of Federal jobs to competition. The result is that government provides better results at lower costs to taxpayers.

OPENING MARKETS

"The trade agenda reflects my strong commitment to open markets around the world for the benefit of American workers, farmers, and businesses. I also am committed to open markets to provide lower prices and greater choices for US consumers and industries. Open trade fuels the engine of economic growth that creates new jobs and new income in the United States and around the world." – President George W. Bush, May 10, 2001

THE ACCOMPLISHMENTS

Opening Markets for American Goods

- *Exports have reached record levels* during the Bush Presidency.

- President Bush, working closely with Congress, *won Trade Promotion Authority to enable quicker passage of trade agreements*. This was the first time Congress approved Trade Promotion Authority in eight years.

- The Bush Administration has *completed free trade agreements with 12 countries*, including Australia, Morocco, Bahrain, Chile, Singapore, and Jordan, and is negotiating free trade agreements with 10 others.

- The Administration is in the process of forming a Free Trade Area of the Americas, which will become *the world's largest free trade area*.

- The Administration played a critical leadership role in *successfully launching a new round of global trade negotiations* at the World Trade Organization (WTO).

- The Bush Administration developed an aggressive plan to open international markets for US farmers – which helped generate a *10 percent increase in agricultural exports between 2000 and 2003*.

- The President signed a *major expansion of assistance to help workers displaced by trade to acquire new skills and find new jobs*. The Trade Act of 2003 nearly tripled the Trade Adjustment Assistance program. In 2003 it provided some $1.3 billion in training and income support, with nearly 200,000 workers eligible for assistance.

- President Bush is *ensuring that our trading partners abide by their international commitments by aggressively enforcing our trade laws*. For example, the Administration brought the first-ever WTO case against China for its discriminatory tax treatment against US semiconductor makers. In July 2004, China agreed to end this unfair practice.

EXPANDING
HOMEOWNERSHIP

"This Administration will constantly strive to promote an ownership society in America. We want more people owning their own home. It is in our national interest that more people own their own home. After all, if you own your own home, you have a vital stake in the future of our country." – President George W. Bush, December 16, 2003

THE ACCOMPLISHMENTS

Increasing Homeownership

- The US *homeownership rate reached a record 69.2 percent* in the second quarter of 2004. The number of homeowners in the United States reached 73.4 million, the most ever. And for the first time, the majority of minority Americans own their own homes.

- The President set a goal to *increase the number of minority homeowners by 5.5 million families by the end of the decade*. Through his homeownership challenge, the President called on the private sector to help in this effort. More than two dozen companies and organizations have made commitments to increase minority homeownership – including pledges to provide more than $1.1 trillion in mortgage purchases for minority homebuyers this decade.

- President Bush *signed the $200 million-per-year American Dream Downpayment Act* which will help approximately 40,000 families each year with their downpayment and closing costs.

- The Administration proposed the *Zero-Downpayment Initiative* to allow the Federal Housing Administration to insure mortgages for first-time homebuyers without a downpayment. Projections indicate this could generate over 150,000 new homeowners in the first year alone.

- President Bush proposed a new Single Family Affordable Housing Tax Credit to *increase the supply of affordable homes*.

- The President has proposed to *more than double funding for the Self-Help Homeownership Opportunity Program* (SHOP), where government and non-profit organizations work closely together to increase homeownership opportunities.

- The President proposed $2.7 billion in USDA home loan guarantees to support rural homeownership and $1.1 billion in direct loans for low-income borrowers unable to secure a mortgage through a conventional lender. These loans are expected to *provide 42,800 homeownership opportunities to rural families across America*.

ENERGY SECURITY

"Our objective [should be] to avoid any crisis in the first instance. This requires a four-part strategy. First, to make energy security a priority of our foreign policy, by restoring American credibility with overseas suppliers and building strong relationships with energy-producing nations in our hemisphere. Second, to encourage environmentally-friendly exploration and production of domestic energy sources, like oil, natural gas and coal. Third, to promote the production of electricity, to keep pace with America's growing demands. Fourth, to support the development of cost-effective alternative energy sources. The goals of this strategy are clear, to ensure a steady supply of affordable energy for America's homes and businesses and industries, and to work toward the day when America achieves energy independence." – President George W. Bush, March 2, 2001

THE ACCOMPLISHMENTS

Long-term Energy Plan

- President Bush put forward *the first comprehensive, long-term energy plan in a decade* to promote affordable, reliable, and secure energy supplies through conservation, investment in new technology, and finding and producing new domestic sources of energy.

- *The Bush Administration has completed, or is in the process of implementing, nearly 75 percent of the 106 recommendations contained in the President's comprehensive National Energy Policy,* such as filling the Strategic Petroleum Reserve to 700 million barrels.

- President Bush also proposed *modernizing the electricity grid* by reforming outdated laws, opening access to the transmission grid, establishing regional planning and coordination, and establishing mandatory reliability standards to prevent blackouts.

- *The President has advocated funding clean coal research and increasing use of clean coal technology;* new efficiency standards for Federal and state governments and consumer products; tax incentives for use of renewable sources of energy like wind and solar power; and opening a small area (less than one percent) of the Arctic National Wildlife Refuge for oil and gas exploration. The Arctic National Wildlife Refuge has the potential to provide over one million barrels of oil a day and provides access to one of the largest known reserves of natural gas in the United States.

- President Bush launched a *groundbreaking initiative to develop technologies and infrastructure to produce, store, and distribute hydrogen* for use in fuel-cell vehicles, electricity generation, and other applications. Hydrogen-powered fuel cells will be able to power cars, trucks, homes, and businesses while producing virtually no pollution or greenhouse gases.

- The President has proposed *tax incentives for the purchase of fuel-efficient hybrid vehicles*.

- President Bush proposed *extending the ethanol tax credit* to encourage its continued use as an alternative source of fuel, and promoted the safe expansion of nuclear energy, one of the cleanest forms of energy generation.

CORPORATE ACCOUNTABILTY REFORM

"My Administration pressed for greater corporate integrity. A united Congress has written it into law. And today I sign the most far-reaching reforms of American business practices since the time of Franklin Delano Roosevelt. This new law sends very clear messages that all concerned must heed. This law says to every dishonest corporate leader: you will be exposed and punished; the era of low standards and false profits is over; [and] no boardroom in America is above or beyond the law." – President George W. Bush, July 30, 2002

THE ACCOMPLISHMENTS

Greater Corporate Accountability

- President Bush signed *the most sweeping corporate accountability reforms since Franklin Roosevelt*.

- The President created the Corporate Fraud Task Force to *investigate and prosecute corporate fraud*. Federal prosecutors have filed more than 400 corporate fraud cases, charged over 900 defendants, including more than 60 corporate CEOs and company presidents, with a crime involving corporate fraud, and secured convictions or guilty pleas against more than 500 of these defendants.

- The Security and Exchange Commission's (SEC) enforcement division has *filed almost 800 enforcement actions for violations of the Federal securities laws* and sought to bar a record number of directors and officers from serving in leadership capacities of public companies.

- The SEC has also *responded swiftly to the mutual fund abuses* that came to light last year. The SEC filed 41 enforcement actions related to the abuse, obtaining close to $1 billion in penalties, which will be returned to investors.

Protecting Consumer Privacy

- In order to combat the problem of identity theft, one of the fastest growing financial crimes, President Bush signed the Identity Theft Penalty Enhancement Act, *which dramatically strengthens the fight against identity theft and fraud*. The law also prescribes prison sentences for those who use identity theft to commit other crimes, including terrorism.

- President Bush helped launch *the national "Do Not Call" Registry*. More than 62 million phone numbers have been registered.

- Millions of America's consumers, businesses, and families have been *provided legal protection against unsolicited commercial e-mail* through the Controlling the Assault of Non-Solicited Pornography and Marketing Act of 2003 (CAN-SPAM Act).

IMMIGRATION REFORM

"[O]ver the generations we have received energetic, ambitious, optimistic people from every part of the world. By tradition and conviction, our country is a welcoming society. America is a stronger and better nation because of the hard work and the faith and entrepreneurial spirit of immigrants. Every generation of immigrants has reaffirmed the wisdom of remaining open to the talents and dreams of the world. And every generation of immigrants has reaffirmed our ability to assimilate newcomers – which is one of the defining strengths of our country." – President George W. Bush, January 7, 2004

THE ACCOMPLISHMENTS

More Rational and Humane Immigration Laws

- President Bush proposed a Temporary Worker Program, _reforming immigration laws to be more rational and humane_ by addressing the problems and dangers faced by undocumented workers and reflecting the economic needs of the country.

- The President's proposal would _match willing foreign workers with willing American employers when no American can be found to fill the job._

- Immigration reform would _offer legal temporary worker status to undocumented men and women employed in the United States_ as of January 7, 2004, and to those in foreign countries who have been offered employment here. These workers will be protected by American labor laws, able to obtain legal documents, and able to deal openly with authorities.

- The President has proposed _financial incentives for workers to return to their home countries_ after their work period has expired.

- President Bush is _opposed to amnesty._ Illegal workers will not be given unfair advantage in the citizenship process. The temporary worker program preserves the citizenship path for those who follow the normal application process while bringing millions of hardworking men and women out of the shadows of American life.

- The Bush Administration has _increased the size of our Border Patrol by more than 1,000 new agents._ The size of the Patrol on the northern border between ports of entry has nearly tripled. And the Border Patrol is also installing monitoring devices along the borders to detect illegal activity.

- The President proposed a five-year, $560 million _plan to reduce the backlog of immigration applications_ to bring processing time to 180 days.

- President Bush signed an Executive Order to allow _expedited naturalization for active-duty military personnel._

REFORMING AND MODERNIZING
HEALTH CARE

"With the Medicare Act of 2003, our government is finally bringing prescription drug coverage to the seniors of America. With this law, we're giving older Americans better choices and more control over their health care, so they can receive the modern medical care they deserve.... Our nation has made a promise, a solemn promise to America's seniors. We have pledged to help our citizens find affordable medical care in the later years of life. Lyndon Johnson established that commitment by signing the Medicare Act of 1965. And today, by reforming and modernizing this vital program, we are honoring the commitments of Medicare to all our seniors." – President George W. Bush, December 8, 2003

THE ACCOMPLISHMENTS

Reforming Medicare and Providing a Prescription Drug Benefit

- *For the first time in Medicare's history, a prescription drug benefit will be offered to more than 40 million seniors and disabled Americans, and seniors will hold the power to choose the health care coverage that is best for them.*

- *Millions of seniors already are getting real savings on their prescription drug expenses by using a Medicare-approved drug discount card.* It includes a $600 annual subsidy for low-income Medicare beneficiaries as part of the transitional relief.

- Beginning in 2006, seniors will be able to join Medicare-approved prescription drug plans or get prescription coverage through regular Medicare. *Beneficiaries who now lack coverage will cut their yearly drug costs roughly in half.*

- The new Medicare law provides *greater drug savings to seniors with low incomes*, reducing costs to as little as $2 or $5 per prescription.

- *Medicare will now pick up 95 percent of the cost for beneficiaries with high out-of-pocket drug costs* once they have spent $3,600 on their prescriptions.

- To encourage employers to continue providing important drug benefits, the new Medicare law will *subsidize employer-sponsored retiree benefits*, beginning in 2006.

- Beneficiaries who do not have employer-sponsored coverage can remain enrolled in the traditional Medicare program with or without the new Medicare-approved prescription drug plan or they can sign up for a private Medicare Advantage plan that includes prescription drug coverage. These private plans will compete for seniors' business by *providing better coverage at affordable prices* through marketplace competition, not government price-setting.

Other Improvements in Medicare Coverage

- Medicare's coverage of preventive services is being expanded to *include screenings for cardiovascular disease and diabetes* beginning next year.

- Everyone who enrolls in Medicare beginning next year will be *covered for an initial physical examination.*

- For the first time, Medicare will offer disease management services that will *help some beneficiaries with chronic medical conditions avoid dangerous and costly medical complications*.

Establishing Health Savings Accounts

- The Medicare legislation also *created Health Savings Accounts* (HSAs), tax-free savings accounts that can be used to pay for medical expenses and that will give millions of Americans access to affordable health coverage with more choices, more freedom, and more control over their health decisions.

- HSAs will *allow more Americans to save for health care needs* and will allow more small businesses to help workers secure affordable health coverage.

Access to Needed Coverage and Care

- President Bush signed the *first-ever refundable health insurance tax credit for workers displaced by trade*. The credit covers 65 percent of an eligible worker's health premium for qualifying health insurance.

- President Bush proposed an innovative $70.1 billion *tax credit to make health insurance coverage affordable for millions of uninsured low-income and middle-income Americans*.

- *Funding for health centers has been dramatically increased*, as part of the President's commitment to open or expand 1,200 health center sites to serve an additional 6.1 million people by 2006. Today there are more than 600 new or expanded health centers serving 3 million additional Americans. The populations these health centers serve include the uninsured, low-income individuals, migrant farm workers, and the homeless.

- *Eligibility for coverage has been extended to an estimated 2.6 million low-income Americans* through Medicaid and the State Child Health Insurance Program (SCHIP).

Funding New Medical Research

- The President *doubled the budget for the National Institutes of Health (NIH)*.

Addressing Rising Health Care Costs and Improving Health Care Quality

- President Bush proposed medical liability reform to *reduce frivolous lawsuits* that drive up costs, raise the cost of medical liability insurance, and reduce access to care.

- The Bush Administration announced a new rule *improving access to generic drugs and lowering prescription drug costs for millions of Americans*. The final rule is expected to lead to at least $35 billion over 10 years in drug savings.

- The President has called for greater adoption of electronic medical records, and *set a goal that a majority of Americans have electronic medical records within a decade*. Personal electronic medical records will help save lives, improve health care quality, and may reduce health care costs. The President proposed doubling, to $100 million, grants to test health information technologies.

- In order to *ensure that health professionals give patients the right drugs at the appropriate dosages*, a regulation requiring bar codes on the labels of thousands of drugs and biological products has been implemented.

IMPROVING AMERICAN EDUCATION

"[T]oday begins a new era, a new time in public education in our country. As of this hour, America's schools will be on a new path of reform, and a new path of results. Our schools will have higher expectations. We believe every child can learn. Our schools will have greater resources to help meet those goals. Parents will have more information about the schools, and more say in how their children are educated. From this day forward, all students will have a better chance to learn, to excel, and to live out their dreams." – President George W. Bush, January 8, 2002

THE ACCOMPLISHMENTS

Requiring Accountability

- President Bush, working closely with Republicans and Democrats, *achieved significant and historic education reform with the No Child Left Behind Act*, which promotes student achievement, accountability, and greater choices for parents.

- For the first time, all 50 states, the District of Columbia, and Puerto Rico have *accountability plans for measuring progress in educating America's children*.

- For the first time, *children in grades 3-8 will be tested every year on basic reading and math skills to measure their progress*.

- Annual test results are now published so *parents can measure school performance and statewide progress, and evaluate the quality of their child's school, the qualifications of teachers, and student progress in key subjects*.

- Statewide reports *reveal progress for all student groups*.

- According to a March 2004 study by the Council of Great City Schools, *the achievement gap in both math and reading between African Americans and whites, and Hispanics and whites, is narrowing*.

Ensuring Schools Have Funding and Flexibility to Improve

- Federal spending on education has increased by $15 billion (including the FY 2005 request) – *an increase of almost 40 percent since 2001*.

- Title I funding to America's most needy public schools *increased by $4.6 billion* since 2001.

- President Bush has requested a *75 percent increase in funding for special education* since 2001.

Giving Parents Options

- No Child Left Behind expands options for parents with children in chronically under-performing schools. President Bush believes that no child should be forced to stay in a bad school. *Parents now can choose to send their children to a better-performing public or charter school*.

- For the first time, _Federal Title I funds are required to be used to provide supplemental educational services_ – including tutoring, after school services, and summer school programs – for children in under-performing schools.

- Parents, educators, and community leaders have far _more opportunities than ever before to open charter schools_.

- The Bush Administration worked with Congress to pass the _D.C. School Choice program, providing scholarships to low-income students to expand their options for education_.

Supporting Teachers

- _Spending on programs designed to improve teacher quality has reached almost $3 billion under the Bush Administration_. This allows local school districts to use Federal funds to hire new teachers, increase teacher pay, and improve teacher training and development.

- President Bush sought _special tax help for teachers_ who spend their own money in the classroom.

- The President has fought to _protect teachers from lawsuits_ when they take common-sense action to keep order in the classroom and protect students from violence and disruptive children.

- President Bush proposed _increased loan forgiveness_ – from $5,000 to $17,500 – for math, science, and special education teachers who teach in high-need schools.

Supporting and Improving Head Start

- Including the President's 2005 request, funding for Head Start has _increased by $750 million_.

- _Significant improvements to Head Start have been proposed, including a new focus on preparing children for school_. And a National Reporting System has been established to determine which Head Start centers are preparing children for school and which ones are not.

- _Training in early learning has been provided to more than 50,000 Head Start teachers_.

- The Bush Administration has proposed _giving states greater opportunity to coordinate Head Start, state Pre-K programs, and child care programs_.

Reading First

- To ensure that every child learns to read by the third grade, the President _proposed and signed into law the Reading First program_. This program has already provided more than $2.5 billion to train over 73,000 teachers in effective reading instruction.

Higher Education

- _A record level of assistance is being given to college students_ in the form of Federal loans, grants, and work-study programs.

- _Funding for Pell grants increased 47 percent_. As funding rose by $4 billion, the number of Pell recipients has increased by nearly one million.

- President Bush signed an Executive Order *supporting the White House Initiative on Historically Black Colleges and Universities* to help find new ways to strengthen these schools. The President's Board of Advisors on Historically Black Colleges and Universities is helping these schools benefit from Federal programs, obtain private-sector support for their endowments, and build partnerships to strengthen faculty development and cooperative research. And the *President's 2005 budget will meet his goal of increasing funding for minority-serving institutions by 30 percent*.

- The President established an Advisory Commission on Educational Excellence for Hispanic Americans. The Commission provides *reports on the progress of Hispanic Americans in closing the academic achievement gap*, and attaining the goals established by the No Child Left Behind educational blueprint.

A MORE COMPASSIONATE AMERICA

"[W]e have set out to promote the work of community and faith-based charities. We want to encourage the inspired, to help the helper. Government cannot be replaced by charities, but it can welcome them as partners instead of resenting them as rivals. My Administration will put the Federal government squarely on the side of America's armies of compassion. Our plan will not favor religious institutions over non-religious institutions. As President, I'm interested in what is constitutional, and I'm interested in what works. The days of discriminating against religious institutions, simply because they are religious, must come to an end." – President George W. Bush, February 1, 2001

THE ACCOMPLISHMENTS

Supporting Faith-based and Community Charities

- Immediately upon taking office the President established the Office of Faith-Based and Community Initiatives, which rests on a basic principle: _when it sees social needs in America, the Federal government will look to faith-based programs and community groups to help_.

- The President signed an Executive Order to _end discrimination against faith-based groups_, helping bring down barriers that had prevented faith-based organizations from being considered in the Federal grants process. As a result of the President's efforts, more than $1.1 billion in Federal discretionary grants were awarded to faith-based groups in 2003.

- President Bush launched Access to Recovery, a proposed three-year, _$600 million drug treatment voucher initiative_, which will give addicts expanded access to a full range of faith-based and community providers.

- In 2003, the President's _Compassion Capital Fund_ provided $30 million in grants to more than 80 faith-based and community organizations. Nearly $50 million in grants are available in 2004.

- President Bush proposed a three-year, $450 million _initiative to provide mentors for disadvantaged youth, including the children of prisoners_.

- To help former prisoners contribute to society and stay away from crime, the President proposed a four-year, $300 million initiative to _provide job training and placement services, transitional housing assistance, and mentoring to 50,000 former inmates_.

Building on Welfare Reform

- _The largest welfare caseload decline in history occurred between 1996 and 2003_, with the caseload falling 60 percent.

- Building on past welfare reform successes, President Bush has advocated _a plan to help more welfare recipients achieve independence through work_. Welfare recipients would be required to spend 40 hours per week, either working at a job or in a program designed to help them achieve independence.

- The Bush Administration has _provided historically high levels of funding for child care_.

Combating HIV/AIDS Domestically

- President Bush proposed $17.1 billion in spending in his 2005 budget to *expand prevention, care and treatment, and research efforts to combat HIV/AIDS within the United States*.

- The President *proposed more than $2 billion for the Ryan White HIV/AIDS program*, which provides care and treatment for those living with HIV/AIDS, and $2.7 billion for HIV/AIDS research, a 21 percent increase over 2001 funding.

Battling Homelessness

- In 2003, the Bush Administration announced *the largest amount of homeless assistance in history*, $1.27 billion to fund 3,700 local housing and service programs around the country.

- President Bush has proposed the Samaritan Initiative, *a new $70 million program to provide supportive services and housing for chronically homeless individuals*.

- The Interagency Council on Homelessness has been revitalized, *bringing together 20 Federal agencies to coordinate efforts to end chronic homelessness in 10 years*.

Helping Americans with Disabilities

- President Bush announced the New Freedom Initiative to *promote the full participation of people with disabilities in all areas of society* by increasing access to assistive technologies, expanding educational and employment opportunities, and promoting full access to community life.

- President Bush requested *the largest increases of any President in history for the Individuals with Disabilities Education Act*, securing more than $3.7 billion in additional funding since 2001.

- The President fulfilled his promise to fully implement requirements that *all Federal government electronic and information technologies be accessible to individuals with disabilities*.

- The President proposed $739 million through 2009 to *remove transportation barriers still faced by individuals with disabilities* and has obtained $20 million in matching grants to help people with disabilities buy equipment for telecommuting to work.

Fostering a Culture of Service and Citizenship

- In his 2002 State of the Union address the President announced *the USA Freedom Corps to foster a culture of service, citizenship, and responsibility*. In less than three years the USA Freedom Corps, the largest clearinghouse of volunteer service opportunities ever created, has enlisted millions of new volunteers.

- This year AmeriCorps, the domestic service program headed by the Corporation for National and Community Service, *will grow to 75,000 members – a 50 percent increase*.

- *The Peace Corps received its largest budget ever* and has grown to nearly 7,600 volunteers, its highest enrollment in almost three decades.

- *Senior Corps has increased by almost 100,000 members in the last year.* Today, more than a half-million members participate in its three programs: Retired and Senior Volunteer Program, Senior Companions, and Foster Grandparents.

- *Almost two million students have volunteered through the Learn and Serve America* programs, which incorporate community service into academic and extracurricular activities to make service an integral part of education.

- Today, *more than 1,200 local communities have formed Citizen Corps Councils*, which contribute to community emergency preparation, prevention, and response activities.

- *More than 5,000 Americans are serving in the new Medical Reserve Corps.* The Corps brings together volunteers trained in medicine, who will assist emergency response teams during large-scale medical emergencies.

- *There are more than 9,700 registered Neighborhood Watch programs*, which have been expanded to incorporate terrorism prevention and education into their existing crime prevention mission.

- *Participants in Volunteers in Police Service (VIPS) have increased 900 percent*, and over 50,000 people have completed Community Emergency Response Team (CERT) training.

PROTECTING CHILDREN,
STRENGTHENING FAMILIES

"The safety and well-being of our children is a shared priority for all Americans and Federal, state, and local authorities. We must use every available resource to find and safely return missing children to their families and their homes, and we must use every available tool to vigorously prosecute and severely punish those who would do our children harm." – President George W. Bush, April 10, 2003

THE ACCOMPLISHMENTS

Protecting Children

- President Bush signed the PROTECT Act in April 2003, which *gives law enforcement new tools to prevent, investigate, and prosecute violent crimes against children and increases punishment for Federal crimes against children*.

- President Bush instituted a national initiative to *expand and coordinate the AMBER Alert system*, which notifies the public about child abductions. Since the President announced his AMBER Alert initiative in October 2002, AMBER Alerts have been credited with helping recover approximately 100 children.

- *Laws against child pornography have been strengthened*. In the last three years, Federal prosecutions for child pornography and exploitation have increased more than 40 percent.

- Operation Predator, *a comprehensive initiative to safeguard children from foreign national pedophiles, human traffickers, international sex tourists, and internet pornographers, was launched*. Operation Predator has resulted in more than 3,200 arrests nationwide and 500 arrests by foreign law enforcement.

- President Bush signed legislation requiring states to *conduct criminal background checks on prospective foster and adoptive parents*.

- A new abstinence initiative *will double the funding for abstinence-only education*; develop model abstinence-only education curricula; review all Federal programming for youth addressing teen pregnancy prevention, family planning, and STD and HIV/AIDS prevention, to ensure that the Federal government is sending consistent health messages to teens; and create a public education campaign designed to help parents communicate with their children about the risks associated with early sexual activity.

- The President announced a *$450 million mentoring initiative* to support schools and non-profit, community, and faith-based organizations in matching disadvantaged children with caring adult mentors.

- The Bush Administration has successfully defended the *Children's Internet Protection Act*, which requires that schools and libraries have internet safety measures in place to filter content that is harmful to minors, in order to receive federal money for internet access. The President also signed the Dot Kids act which designates that ".kids" websites will be safe for children and monitored for content, safety, and objectionable material.

- *Smoking, drinking, and the use of illegal drugs among teenagers all fell between 2001 and 2003*.

Encouraging Safe and Stable Families

- President Bush signed the _Promoting Safe and Stable Families Act_ to help states promote adoption for children in foster care and provide post-adoptive support to families.

- The President signed the _Adoption Promotion Act of 2003_, which provides extra incentives for states to increase adoption of older children.

- _The adoption tax credit increased from $5,000 to $10,000 per child._

- The President has proposed $240 million per year in Federal funds over five years to _support healthy marriages_ through research, demonstration projects and technical assistance on family formation and healthy marriage activities.

- The President has asked for $50 million to fund a _new initiative promoting responsible fatherhood_ by providing low-income fathers with job training, subsidized employment, career-advancing education, skills-based marriage and parenting education, and mentoring.

- _The percentage of high school students who reported ever having had sex was significantly lower in 2003 than in 1991._

- _The divorce rate has fallen steadily for more than a decade._

- The proportion of children in married-parent families rose slightly since 1999 – _the first increase in more than two decades._

- President Bush called on Congress to pass a _Federal Marriage Amendment defining marriage as the union between one man and one woman._

PROMOTING A
CULTURE OF LIFE

"In the debate about the rights of the unborn, we are asked to broaden the circle of our moral concern. We're asked to live out our calling as Americans. We're asked to honor our own standards, announced on the day of our founding in the Declaration of Independence. We're asked by our convictions and tradition and compassion to build a culture of life, and make this a more just and welcoming society." – President George W. Bush, November 5, 2003

THE ACCOMPLISHMENTS

Building a Culture of Life

- *President Bush signed legislation to end partial birth abortion* – a procedure the late Democratic Senator Daniel Patrick Moynihan described as "as close to infanticide as anything I have come upon."

- The President signed the Born Alive Infants Protection Act, which *ensures that every infant born alive, including an infant who survives an abortion procedure, is considered a person under Federal law*.

- The President signed the Unborn Victims of Violence Act, which provides that under Federal law, *any person who causes death or injury to a child in the womb shall be charged with a separate offense, in addition to any charges relating to the mother*.

- President Bush restored the Mexico City Policy, which states that *taxpayer funds should not be provided to organizations that pay for abortions or advocate or actively promote abortion, either in the United States or abroad*.

- President Bush's 2005 budget includes $10 million to *support maternity group homes for women in crisis*.

- In August 2001, the President announced his decision to *allow medical research using embryonic stem cells while still respecting and upholding the value and sanctity of human life*. This policy permits, for the first time, Federal funding of research using existing stem cell lines while not sanctioning or encouraging the destruction of additional live human embryos.

- The President *created the President's Council on Bioethics* to study the human and moral ramifications of developments in biomedical and behavioral science and technology.

- President Bush has *called on the Congress to pass a law banning all human cloning*.

- States now have the option to *provide vital health care services to promote healthy pregnancies for women and their unborn children* who would otherwise be ineligible for coverage under the State Children's Health Insurance Program (SCHIP). States are also able to provide eligibility to unborn children of low-income immigrants, which results in access to important prenatal care.

FIGHTING CRIME

"For all our children's sake, this nation must reclaim our neighborhoods and our streets. We need a national strategy to assure that every community is attacking gun violence with focus and intensity. I'm here today to announce a national initiative to help cities like Philadelphia fight gun violence. [My Administration] will establish a network of law enforcement and community initiatives targeted at gun violence... We're going to reduce gun violence in America, and those who commit crimes with guns will find a determined adversary in my Administration." – President George W. Bush, May 14, 2001

THE ACCOMPLISHMENTS

Making America Safer

- Violent crime rates decreased 21 percent between 1999-2000 and 2001-2002. _The violent crime rate is now down to its lowest point in the last three decades_.

- _Property crime dropped 13 percent_ between 1999-2000 and 2001-2002.

- There were about _130,000 fewer victims of gun crime_ in 2001-2002 than there were in 1999-2000, the first two-year period with less than a million gun-crime victims since 1993.

- Since 2001 the _FBI budget has increased 60 percent_.

- The President directed the Department of Justice, as part of Project Safe Neighborhoods, to _prosecute aggressively those who use guns illegally_. The Bush Administration has devoted more than $1 billion to Project Safe Neighborhoods.

- In 2003, the Department of Justice _brought charges against more than 13,000 offenders for Federal firearms crimes_, the highest annual figure on record. In the past three years, Federal prosecutions of gun crime have increased 68 percent.

- The Bush Administration proposed and is implementing Project Child Safe to _help provide free trigger locks to all handgun owners_.

- The President _supports the bipartisan Crime Victims' Rights Amendment_, ensuring that victims of violent crime have the right to be notified of public proceedings involving the crime, to be heard at public proceedings regarding the criminal's sentence or potential release, to have their safety considered, and to have consideration of their claims of restitution.

- President Bush proposed the Advancing Justice Through DNA Technology initiative, with $1 billion in funding over five years to _identify criminals quickly and accurately, protect the innocent from wrongful prosecution, and help identify missing persons_. The initiative will help eliminate backlogs of unanalyzed DNA samples, improve laboratory capacity, stimulate research and development, and provide training in the collection and use of DNA evidence.

- The President signed the _Law Enforcement Officers Safety Act_ exempting law enforcement officers from state laws prohibiting the carrying of concealed firearms.

Helping Victims of Domestic Violence

- The Bush Administration has secured *historic levels of funding for programs that prosecute offenders and protect women against domestic violence*.

- Twenty million dollars in grants have been awarded to help communities establish and support Family Justice Centers across America, which will *provide domestic violence victims and their families comprehensive services*.

Cutting Drug Use and Increasing Drug Treatment

- *Youth drug use declined by more than 10 percent* between 2001 and 2003, meaning 400,000 fewer young people used drugs.

- Recent use of ecstasy, which sharply increased between 1998 and 2001, *fell by half* among middle and high school students between 2001 and 2003, and recent use of LSD *fell by almost two-thirds*.

- The Bush Administration launched Access to Recovery – *an initiative to provide drug treatment to individuals otherwise unable to obtain access to services*. People in need of treatment receive an assessment of their treatment need and are issued vouchers to obtain help at effective treatment organizations, including faith-based and community facilities.

- President Bush proposed $25 million – a $23 million increase – to *help schools develop and implement student drug testing programs*.

Ending Racial Profiling

- Less than six weeks after taking office, President Bush called for *an end to racial profiling in Federal law enforcement*. He is the first President to do so. And the Adminstration has implemented specific guidelines prohibiting the practice in Federal law enforcement.

STRENGTHENING THE JUDICIARY

"A President has fewer greater responsibilities than that of nominating men and women to the courts of the United States. A Federal judge holds a position of great influence and respect, and can hold it for a lifetime. When a President chooses a judge, he is placing in human hands the authority and majesty of the law. He owes it to the Constitution and to the country to choose with care.... My nominees today and in the years to come will be notable for their distinction and accomplishments. And all will be exceptional for their humanity and their integrity." – President George W. Bush, May 9, 2001

THE ACCOMPLISHMENTS

Choosing Outstanding Nominees for the Judiciary

- President Bush has appointed individuals who clearly understand *the role of a judge is to interpret the law, not to legislate from the bench*.

- The President has *nominated 51 individuals to the Federal courts of appeals and 174 individuals to the Federal district courts* (as of August 2004).

- These nominees come from diverse backgrounds and share *sterling credentials and the highest standards of legal training, character, and judgment* – 99 percent have been rated either well-qualified or qualified by the American Bar Association.

- One non-partisan study conducted last year concluded, based on a review of American Bar Association ratings, that *the President's nominees are "the most qualified appointees" of any recent Administration*.

CONSERVING AND PROTECTING
THE ENVIRONMENT

"Our duty is to use the land well, and sometimes, not to use it at all. This is our responsibility as citizens; but, more than that, it is our calling as stewards of the Earth. Good stewardship of the environment is not just a personal responsibility, it is a public value. Americans are united in the belief that we must preserve our natural heritage and safeguard the land around us." – President George W. Bush, May 30, 2001

THE ACCOMPLISHMENTS

Improving our Environment

- *Our air is cleaner, our drinking water is purer, and our land is better protected and cared for than it was four years ago*.

Improving Air Quality

- President Bush proposed the Clear Skies Initiative, an effort to aggressively *reduce air pollution from power plants by 70 percent and improve air quality throughout the country*.

- The President proposed requiring the *steepest emissions cuts in over a decade for coal-burning power plants*. The Clean Air Interstate Rule, modeled after the Clear Skies Initiative, will require power plants to substantially reduce emissions of sulfur dioxide and nitrogen oxide. Sulfur dioxide emissions will be cut by nearly 70 percent and nitrogen oxide emissions will be cut by approximately 50 percent.

- President Bush proposed the Clean Air Mercury Rule that *will regulate mercury emissions from power plants for the first time*, imposing a mandatory 70 percent cut by 2018.

- The Clean Air Nonroad Diesel Rule *requires that emission levels from construction, agricultural, and industrial diesel-powered equipment be dramatically cut*. This new rule requires that soot and nitrogen oxide emission be reduced by more than 90 percent and the sulfur content of diesel fuel be cut by 99 percent.

- President Bush is committed to *reducing greenhouse gas emissions by 18 percent over the next 10 years*.

Promoting Healthy Forests

- The Healthy Forests Initiative is *helping to prevent catastrophic fires* by managing forests with controlled burns, cleaning out the underbrush, and thinning the areas that are vulnerable to intense fires and insect attacks. Controlling forest fires will help save the lives of firefighters, save communities, and protect threatened and endangered species.

Restoring and Protecting our Nation's Lands

- In January 2002, President Bush signed historic legislation that *will accelerate the cleanup and redevelopment of contaminated, underutilized industrial sites* known as brownfields. More than 1,000 brownfields already have been restored – which is more than were restored in the previous seven years.

- The President announced an aggressive new national goal to *create, improve, and protect at least three million wetland acres* over the next five years.

- President Bush signed into law a farm bill providing nearly $40 billion over a decade to *restore millions of acres of wetlands, protect habitats, conserve water, and improve streams and rivers* near working farms and ranches.

Improving our National Parks

- To meet his commitment to *improving park maintenance and construction*, the President proposed spending almost $5 billion over five years. The FY 2005 request is a 37 percent increase over FY 2001.

- President Bush supports a $7.8 billion Comprehensive Everglades Restoration Plan that will *restore millions of acres in the Everglades* and ensure that South Florida has a reliable supply of fresh water.

Making our Nation's Energy Supply Clean and Secure

- President Bush proposed $1.7 billion in research funding to *develop clean, hydrogen-powered automobiles* and infrastructure technologies.

- The Bush Administration supports increasing automobile fuel economy and encouraging new technologies that reduce our dependence on imported oil. For the first time in a decade, *the Administration raised Corporate Average Fuel Economy (CAFE) standards for SUVs, vans, and light pick-up trucks*.

- The President has proposed *tax incentives for the purchase of fuel-efficient hybrid vehicles*.

- The President has proposed $4.1 billion in tax incentives to *spur the use of clean and renewable energy*, and energy-efficient technologies.

Improving the Conservation of Oceans and the Quality of Water

- The President proposed $21 million for the Water 2025 Initiative to help states, tribes, and local communities in the West *improve conservation and better monitor local resources*.

THE CONDITION OF AMERICA

Citizens rightly judge a President on the proposals he makes and the laws he signs. Yet there is another standard they judge by as well: the economic and social condition of the country. Are things in America getting better, or worse? Is progress being made, or lost? Are social indicators improving, or declining? With that in mind, it may be useful to provide a brief summary of the condition of America, based on recent empirical data.

Economic Indicators

- Since last summer, the American economy has grown at the fastest rate of any major industrialized nation.

- America's economy has been growing at rates as fast as any in nearly 20 years.

- Nearly 1.5 million jobs have been created since August 2003 and 1.3 million new jobs have been created this year alone. The unemployment rate today is *below* the average unemployment rate of the 1970s, the 1980s, and the 1990s.

- From 2000 to 2003, productivity grew at the fastest three-year rate in more than a half-century, raising the standard of living for all Americans.

- The Conference Board's index of leading indicators has risen at an average annual rate of 4.2 percent since March 2003 – the fastest 15-month period of increase in 20 years – suggesting vibrant economic growth in the near term.

- The stock market has regained more than $4 trillion in equity since its low in mid-2002. In 2003 the Dow Jones Industrial Average rose 25 percent and the NASDAQ rose 50 percent.

- Manufacturing activity expanded in July 2004 for the 14th consecutive month.

- Real after-tax incomes are up 11 percent since December 2000.

- Interest rates reached their lowest levels in decades during the Bush Administration.

- Homeownership is at its highest level ever and mortgage rates reached their lowest level in decades during the Bush Administration. And for the first time, the majority of minority Americans own their own homes.

- During the Bush Presidency, the United States has experienced one of the lowest core inflation rates (averaging two percent per year) in the past 40 years.

Crime and Drug Use

- Violent crime rates decreased 21 percent between 1999-2000 and 2001-2002. The violent crime rate is now down to its lowest point in the last three decades.

- Property crime dropped 13 percent between 1999-2000 and 2001-2002.

- There were about 130,000 fewer victims of gun crime in 2001-2002 than there were in 1999-2000, the first two-year period with less than a million gun-crime victims since 1993.

- Smoking, drinking, and illegal drug use among teenagers all fell between 2001 and 2003.

- Between 2001 and 2003, teen drug use fell by more than 10 percent – the first decline of such magnitude in more than a decade.

- Recent use of ecstasy, which sharply increased between 1998 and 2001, fell by half among high school students – and past use of LSD fell by almost two-thirds.

Welfare

- The largest welfare caseload decline in history occurred between 1996 and 2003, with the caseload falling 60 percent.

Education

- According to a March 2004 study by the Council of Great City Schools, the achievement gap in both math and reading between African Americans and whites, and Hispanics and whites, is narrowing.

- The high school dropout rate and the number of teens neither enrolled in school nor working was lower in 2001 than in 1996.

- More African Americans today are finishing high school, going to college, and earning higher salaries than ever. Since 1980 the percentage of African Americans earning high school diplomas has increased by more than 27 percent. And according to the Census Bureau, less than eight percent of African Americans had completed four years of college in 1980 – compared to 17 percent who had a bachelor's degree in 2002.

Family Life

- The divorce rate has fallen steadily for more than a decade.

- The proportion of children in married-parent families rose slightly since 1999 – the first increase in more than two decades.

- The percentage of high school students who reported ever having had sex was significantly lower in 2003 than in 1991.

Other

- Alcohol-related traffic fatalities are near their lowest level since the government began keeping such statistics.

- The rate of teen deaths by accident, homicide, and suicide fell 17 percent between 1996 and 2001.

- In 2002 the number of teens who smoked cigarettes daily dropped to the lowest point since data were first collected.

Printed in the USA
CPSIA information can be obtained
at www.ICGtesting.com
JSHW052020140824
68134JS00027B/2565